Under the Mushroom Cloud

by
Anne Schraff

Perfection Learning Corporation

Logan, Iowa 51546

Cover Illustration: Carlotta M. Tormey

For information, contact:
Perfection Learning Corporation
1000 North Second Avenue, P.O. Box 500,
Logan, Iowa 51546-0500.
Tel: 1-800-831-4190 • Fax: 1-800-543-2745
RLB ISBN-13: 978-0-7569-0623-8
RLB ISBN-10: 0-7569-0623-7
PB ISBN-13: 978-0-7891-5555-9
PB ISBN-10: 0-7891-5555-9
4 5 6 7 8 9 PP 12 11 10 09 08 07
perfectionlearning.com
Printed in the U.S.A.

1 "Here we are," said Daniel Robinson's dad.
"Where?" Kevane, Daniel's brother, asked.

Sixteen-year-old Daniel had never been in such a remote wilderness. He had sat in the backseat of their off-road vehicle and watched out the window as they bounced and bumped over miles of dirt roads. Finally they had come to a meadow in the shadow of the White Ranch mountains. Daniel's mom and dad described it as "beautiful," but Daniel just thought it looked like a bunch of grass and trees.

"Just think," his dad marveled as he stepped out of the car, "ours are probably the first human feet to step on this grass in ages."

"Maybe that should tell us something," Daniel said saracastically. His brother agreed. Neither boy was very excited about the trip. They didn't care too much about seeing deer drinking from streams or black bears bustling off through the woods. But they knew their parents hadn't brought their teenage boys camping just to give them a wilderness experience. They had also retreated from society to come to a decision. In this quiet, unhurried place the Robinsons had to decide what to do about Arthur.

Daniel's dad had been a Big Brother to seven-year-old Arthur now for a year. He took the boy to baseball games and movies. Daniel didn't mind his dad sharing hot dogs with the kid at the amusement park, but it was getting out of hand. Arthur was a ward of the state, and now Daniel's mom and dad wanted to adopt him.

"We need to do it as a family, though," Mr. Robinson had said. "It can't just be your mother's and my decision. You guys have to go along with it too. Otherwise it's not fair to you, and it's not fair to Arthur either."

Daniel's mom had nodded, her expression serious. "Yes. We either take Arthur as our son or give him the chance to find another family who'll love him.

Time is running out for that little boy. He's dangerously close to growing up without a family."

Daniel wasn't so sure it was a good idea for the family to adopt Arthur. He thought everybody was getting along pretty well now, so why bring in a moody little kid with lots of problems? Arthur had lost his mother when he was a baby, and he never knew his father. He had spent time in a dozen foster homes, and he had behavioral problems at school. He was a pretty nice kid most of the time, Daniel had to admit, and Daniel's mom had already fallen in love with him. But Daniel had enough trouble dealing with his 14-year-old brother without bringing a 7-year-old with a temper into the mix.

Daniel thought Kevane felt the same way about the situation. A couple of weeks ago their mom had talked Daniel and Kevane into taking Arthur to the swimming pool. They had arrived during one of the hourly breaks. No kids were allowed to get back into the pool until the lifeguards blew their whistles. Arthur didn't understand and went running toward the empty pool. Kevane had to chase after him, and when he caught the little guy, the kid threw a temper tantrum until break time was over. It was just too much of a hassle having Arthur around. Daniel just couldn't see how anybody in the family would be better off with Arthur in the house.

But Daniel's mom and dad had decided that what the family needed to make that final decision was some together time in the mountains without distractions—no television, no Internet, and no phone. His parents thought everyone would be able to think clearly in the mountains.

While Mr. Robinson set up the tents, Daniel nudged Kevane.

"Let's go look around," he said.

"Sounds good," Kevane answered. "I'm in no hurry for our big family conference."

"Hey, Dad," Daniel said. "We're going to take a little hike."

"Good idea," Mr. Robinson said. "Fresh air will clear your minds. We'll talk when you get back. I'll get some steaks on a fire once these tents are put up."

The boys began walking toward the

woods. With only two years separating the brothers, the boys seemed to have a love-hate relationship. They could fight and argue like enemies one minute, and the next minute they could get along like best friends.

"Man," Kevane said, looking up at a lodgepole pine, "look how tall and straight that old tree is."

"Yeah," Daniel said. There were so many pine needles on the ground that the boys bounced a little when they walked. They had walked about four miles from camp, and now they stood in a valley near the huge granite shoulder of mesalike mountains. Daniel remembered reading in the newspaper about heavy rains that had hit the mountains in the spring. He noticed some long-buried stones that were now uncovered.

"Feels funny right here, like I'm standing on wood," Kevane said, stopping.

"It's the carpet of pine needles," Daniel said. "They're pretty thick."

Kevane shook his head. "No, it's something else." He knelt down, and using his knife, he scraped away the dirt until he hit something. "There's something here," he said. "Something weird."

"Like what, Agent Mulder?" Daniel asked with a skeptical grin on his face. Kevane had a vivid imagination. He was addicted to the TV show *The X-Files*, and Daniel knew watching that show made his imagination run wild.

Kevane scraped more. "It looks like a . . . door," he said.

"Right," Daniel said. Nonetheless, he was curious. So he joined his brother in scraping away the dirt until they had uncovered a door about three feet by three feet.

"Hey, look!" Kevane cried. "A rusty handle! The door must open and lead somewhere!"

"Yeah, right," Daniel laughed. "Come on, some guy dumped some trash here. The junk door was probably covered up until those heavy rains hit last spring. It's probably been there for a hundred years. It doesn't lead to some underground world like on your TV shows!"

Kevane grabbed the handle and tried to pull the door up. Nothing happened.

Daniel laughed harder. "Come on, Kev, there's nothing there but a rotten old door!"

"Come on, Danny, help me! I felt it give a little. I'll tie my belt around the handle, and we'll both pull!" Kevane pleaded, his eyes dancing with excitement.

"Okay, I'll go along with the game, little brother," Daniel said. Both boys used all of their strength to tug at the door handle, and suddenly it lifted up, almost throwing them both over backward.

"Danny!" Kevane gasped when he'd recovered his balance. "There are stairs leading down! Stairs leading into the ground! Will you look at that?"

"It's probably an old root cellar," Daniel scoffed. "In the old days, people kept their vegetables in holes in the ground like that." Still, Daniel had to admit, to himself if not to Kevane, that he *was* surprised to find stairs under the old door.

"Maybe it leads to a cemetery," Kevane said with a chilling tremor in his voice. "Maybe the old miners buried their dead down there. Or maybe it's an old mine shaft."

"Rein in that imagination," Daniel told his brother. "Someone might have mined around here a hundred years ago. There was probably gold in these mountains. But nobody's come around here in a long time. Even the bad road we came in on was just fixed to make it passable. The only way you could get all the way in here would be to use horses or mules . . . It's probably just an old cellar."

"Want to go down and see?" Kevane suggested eagerly. Of the two boys, Kevane was the more daring. When the family had gone to an amusement park a year earlier, Kevane was the one who tried bungee jumping. Daniel didn't like to take chances. Kevane played football with wild abandon, not even giving injuries a thought, but Daniel chose track because he didn't want to collide with monster linebackers every week.

"I don't know, Kev. Who knows what's down there? It could collapse on us," Daniel worried.

"Let's just go a little ways. If things start getting shaky, we'll get out fast," Kevane said.

"I guess we could go down a little ways, just to look around," Daniel said. "The minute we see the piles of petrified potatoes and turnips, we'll come on up."

"I'll go first," Kevane volunteered, already heading down. "Look, the steps are carved from stone. Somebody put a lot of effort into making them."

The boys descended to the bottom of the steps, which ended at a tiny room with stone walls. Beyond it was a door standing ajar.

"Let's just look inside that door," Kevane said.

"I guess," Daniel said, following his brother.

They entered a larger room, about ten feet by ten feet, Daniel guessed. Carved coconut heads hung from iron hooks in the stone walls. There were coconuts carved into tiger and monkey heads, and jewels were used for the eyes, which glowed in the murky darkness. There was enough light coming from the open trapdoor for the boys to see brilliant jade eyes on the tiger and glowing topaz eyes on the monkey nearest them.

"Wow," Kevane cried, "look at all this stuff! It's amazing. I bet those carved heads are worth a lot. The eyes are probably made of real jewels. The stuff in here must be worth a fortune."

Daniel continued to inspect the strange heads that were hanging all around them. He couldn't decide if they were beautiful or hideous—maybe both.

"Somebody must have put all this stuff down here and then abandoned it ages ago. So now it's here for the taking," Kevane said, touching a carved tiger.

"Wait a minute, little brother," Daniel said. "Look at how clean everything is. No cobwebs, no dust. Somebody is taking care of business, you know what I'm saying?"

Kevane looked disappointed but not convinced. "Maybe an underground place like this doesn't get dust and cobwebs." He spotted a small monkey head with striking jade eyes. "Dan, it doesn't make sense that anybody is actually living here in the middle of nowhere, does it?"

Daniel looked across the room. He saw another door, one covered with carvings of eagles, muskrats, squirrels, and bears. It was a beautiful work of art.

Kevane's eyes sparkled with fresh excitement. "Come on, let's open that door and see what's on the other side," he said.

"I don't know," Daniel said. "Maybe we're invading somebody's home. We don't know what we're getting into here. If you came to a big, old house in the middle of nowhere, would you just walk in and start looking around at the stuff?"

Kevane took a deep breath. "So maybe somebody lived here 40 years ago or something, but not now. There's no car or truck or anything parked outside, and that trapdoor we came in through hasn't been opened in a long time. There's no sign of life!"

"Maybe there's another entrance," Daniel said. "We just don't know. We're right up against the mountains. Maybe there's a way to get in through the mountains."

"But it all feels so dead," Kevane argued. "You can feel it when people are around a place. There's nothing here. This stuff is like what you'd find in a sunken ship that's been under the water for a long time." He reached for the monkey head he had been looking at.

"Don't touch anything," Daniel said sharply. "It'd be stealing, and you know it."

Kevane withdrew his hand and returned his attention to the carved door. "I'm going to see if that door opens. I want to see what's on the other side."

Daniel stared at the door. "Kev, we don't even have flashlights," he said. "Listen, we're trespassing. I say we get out of here before we're busted for breaking and entering."

"Aw, don't be such a chicken," Kevane laughed. "I've got plenty of matches in my pocket. I grabbed them in case we wanted to start a campfire of our own. We'll be able to see *something*."

Kevane went to the door and grasped the doorknob, yanking on the door. Suddenly he let out a long howl. Daniel saw him disappear.

2 "Kevane!" Daniel shouted, scrambling to where his brother had been standing. He stopped when he got to a hole in the floor. Daniel dropped to his knees and peered down. He saw Kevane lying in the middle of a straw-covered pit.

"Kevane!" he shouted. "Are you okay? You're not hurt, are you?"

"I'm okay," Kevane said. "I don't think I broke anything."

"Give me your hand," Daniel instructed. "I'll pull you out! Oh, man, I knew we were in over our heads!"

Suddenly Kevane's calm voice crumbled into horror. "Dannnneeee, I think this pit is full of snakes!" he screamed. "Big snakes! They're all over!"

"Give me your hand," Daniel yelled, lying flat and reaching down for Kevane. He grabbed both of his brother's hands and quickly dragged him up out of the pit. Kevane flopped down on the floor, breathing hard.

"You didn't get bitten, did you?" Daniel asked.

"I don't think so, but oh, man, I could see snakes everywhere!" Kevane groaned.

Daniel took a match from Kevane and lit it. By the brief, feeble light, he could only make out a lizard darting around through the straw. Daniel smiled to himself. Lizards looked a lot like snakes in the dark.

"I thought I was done for!" Kevane groaned.

Daniel decided against mentioning that the snake pit his brother had escaped from was just a hole with straw and a sand lizard in it. He'd save that little fact in case he needed some good ammunition sometime.

"Let's just get out of here, Kev. Some weird guy must've built this place so he'd be alone and nobody would bother him. Let's count ourselves lucky to just get out in one piece!" Daniel said.

Kevane looked around the room with the carved heads. Light from beyond the trapdoor illuminated the walls where the animals and birds with their jeweled eyes peered down. He drew near some small carvings of doves with ruby eyes. "I bet there's a fortune right here," Kevane said. "I bet the eyes are real diamonds and rubies and sapphires . . ."

"It's not ours," Daniel said. "Somebody's living here, and the stuff belongs to him. Do we go into our neighbors' houses and rip off their stuff? Now, are you coming, or do I have to drag you out of this place?"

Daniel saw anger flash in Kevane's face. Kevane was a big kid for 14, but when he wrestled with Daniel, he never won. Daniel was bigger and stronger, and he always got the best of Kevane. Daniel knew his brother couldn't stand that.

"I just want to take one of the little birds as a souvenir. What's the big deal about that? Whoever it is will never miss it," Kevane said.

"Leave it alone," Daniel barked. "I mean it. You steal anything, and I'll kick your butt. Quit screwing around, and let's go!"

"You think you're tough, don't you?" Kevane yelled. "You just wait until I'm a little older. We'll see whose butt gets kicked then!"

Daniel pushed Kevane toward the stairs leading to the trapdoor. Daniel started climbing first. Right before he started to climb, Kevane dashed back into the room and grabbed a dove with ruby eyes and stuck it in his pocket. He glanced at Daniel, but Daniel wasn't looking. A satisfied grin spread across Kevane's face as he followed his brother up the steps.

The boys scrambled out of the trapdoor, then closed it the way they had found it. For a moment they stood in the bright sunlight, staring at each other. In a way it was like they had both awakened from the same strange dream.

"Did that really just happen?" Daniel asked, grinning with relief to be out of the underground place.

Kevane touched the dove hiding in his shirt pocket and smiled too. "Yeah, incredible, huh?"

"I'm just glad we got out of there," Daniel said. "Let's get back to camp. Dad's barbecuing steaks, and I don't want to miss that. I'm drooling just thinking about them."

"What do you think is really going on

down there?" Kevane asked as they hiked back toward camp. "Some guy must've built a whole world down there and stored all his treasures. And then what? Maybe he died and left it all . . ."

"Who knows," Daniel said. Although they were a couple miles from camp, he was sure he could smell his dad's barbecue already.

As the boys neared their campsite, Kevane asked, "Are we going to tell Mom and Dad anything about what we found down there?"

Daniel thought about it for a minute. Then he shook his head. "Nah, they'd both be pretty ticked off that we went exploring down that hole. Why should we upset them?"

The truth was that although Daniel did not keep important things from his parents, there were little things he kept to himself. He never told his mom and dad about the time he skipped his last class of the day to go play a new video game at his friend's house. Nor did he tell them that there was a girl in history class named Lisa whom he could not take his eyes off.

There were just some little things, Daniel thought, that parents shouldn't be bothered with.

"Yeah," Kevane agreed. "We'll just not talk about it. They're always after us to be careful and not do stupid things, and I guess going down those stairs was kinda stupid—especially when those snakes almost got me."

"Right," Daniel said with a private chuckle.

They arrived at their campsite and saw that their dad had gotten the tents set up. Their mom was digging in the cooler for their drinks, and their dad was turning the steaks over the open fire.

"See anything exciting?" Mr. Robinson asked his boys.

Kevane and Daniel exchanged glances. "Just the usual," Daniel said. Kevane tried to conceal a smile.

Over their dad's barbecued steaks, the conversation once again turned to Arthur.

"That little boy just needs people to love him," their mom said, her big brown eyes growing misty.

"But the decision has to come from the

whole family," their dad insisted. "We have to know that Arthur will fit into our family and that everybody is committed to making this work. It would be inexcusable to take him and then send him back. He just couldn't handle more rejection."

"I just don't know why you guys want another kid," Kevane said, cutting through the tender steak.

Mr. Robinson had been active with Big Brothers for a long time, and he had helped a lot of fatherless boys, but Arthur seemed to get to him in a special way. "Arthur needs us. I just had the feeling right from the start that he'd gain so much from being in our family, but we'd gain too. This kid has a lot to offer. He'd make us a better, richer family in ways we can't even imagine now," their dad replied.

"Man, do I hear violins playing?" Kevane said.

Their dad frowned. Daniel knew he didn't like wise guys, especially if they were his own sons.

"None of that, Kevane," his dad scolded. "That's just a bad attitude, and I won't have that. You'd better watch yourself that you don't become a selfish person. Maybe it's time both of you boys started looking at things in a different way. Everything isn't all about you guys. Our lives don't just belong to us. They belong to other people too. There's no more bitter and sad person than somebody who has lived just for himself."

Daniel's dad did not preach often, but Daniel thought that when he did, he was pretty good at it. He was good at laying on the guilt.

"Your dad's right," their mom chimed in. "Last Thanksgiving when we helped out at the homeless shelter for a couple of hours, all you boys did was gripe."

"I never dished out more mashed potatoes in my life," Kevane said. "My arm was starting to hurt. It messed up my shoulder so bad I couldn't throw the football the next day."

Nobody said anything after that, but Daniel could see his parents were disappointed in Kevane. Maybe in Daniel too.

After lunch, Daniel and Kevane took off

again. Their dad had told them to look at the rock formations in the area. "Puts life into perspective," he'd said. Before they knew it, the boys were close to the trapdoor again. They hadn't agreed to go there, but they'd just ended up there, standing a few yards from the door and staring at it.

"Want to take another quick look?" Kevane was the first to say what they were both thinking. It was just so incredible, so unusual that neither boy could get it off his mind.

"We better not," Daniel said in a halfhearted voice. "You even said it was stupid to go down there the first time."

"Yeah, I know I said that, but it wouldn't hurt to just go down real quick and see if there was anything else we missed before. I mean, who knows what's down there?" Kevane said.

"Yeah, probably more snakes," Daniel laughed.

Kevane just shuddered.

"Maybe this time we'll run into the guy who lives there. Who knows what he'll do to us," Daniel warned.

"No, I bet it's been abandoned for years, maybe decades," Kevane said. "The only reason it looked pretty clean was that it's underground and the wind doesn't blow stuff around." His voice was racing with excitement. "Let's just go down and take another quick look . . . I, uh . . . got two flashlights in my backpack this time, so we can really look around."

Daniel grinned at his brother. "You little fake! You were plotting all along to go down again," he said.

Kevane laughed. "Come on, Dan. You want another peek too. Admit it! The curiosity is eating you alive!"

Daniel laughed too. He *had* been thinking about the place all through lunch. It had been hard to concentrate on the Arthur conversation after their little discovery. Maybe some incredibly rich guy had carved out his little empire down there. There could be more amazing sights than the room with the carved heads.

"Okay, you win," Daniel said. "But we're just going for a quick look, and then we're out of there. I don't want to hang around until some crazy freak finds us in his domain. And when we've had this last look, it's over. We don't even think about ever going back, right?"

"Yeah, sure, absolutely," Kevane promised.

Kevane led the way to the trapdoor, opening it easily this time and leaning it back. The sunlight lit the stairs before them as they went down.

When they reached the room with the carved heads, Kevane and Daniel threw their flashlight beams on them. The heads looked even more striking. The boys saw intricate carvings they hadn't seen before that looked carved from ivory or jade.

"Man, will you look at this stuff!" Kevane cried.

"What if Arthur were with us right now," Daniel said suddenly. "Imagine what a kick a little kid like him would get out of this. It'd be like the adventure of a lifetime. You know how little kids are. Everything is wilder and more exciting for them."

"You sound like you *want* the kid," Kevane said.

"Nah," Daniel said quickly. "It's just that doing stuff with a little kid is fun sometimes . . ."

"Arthur would be ruining everything for us," Kevane said. "Right now he'd be so scared he'd be wetting his pants, or else he'd be running all over knocking the animal heads off the walls."

"Yeah, you're right," Daniel said. "He'd probably want to play football with the coconut heads."

"We could fool him and tell him those animal heads are real. Remember how you fooled me when I was little, telling me the big roots of the tree near our house were snakes sleeping in the shade?" Kevane said.

"Yeah, it was fun messing with your mind," Daniel said.

Kevane gave his brother a nudge. "Admit it. You're softening on the idea of bringing the kid into our family, aren't you?" he asked.

"Nah, who wants a pesky little brother," Daniel said. "I've already got one. That's all I can handle." He laughed then. He talked as if he really didn't want Arthur.

But he could tell Kevane didn't really believe him. He wasn't sure if he believed it himself.

"Okay," Kevane said, moving through the room. "Here's the door we tried to open before when I fell into the snake pit. I'm not making that mistake again. I'm stepping around it."

They both stepped around the hole in the floor. Then they opened the door and moved slowly into the next room, flashlights trained ahead of them. Both boys let out gasps.

The room was filled with stained glass. There were small stained glass suncatchers hanging on the walls and huge stained glass windows mounted around the room. There were boxes made of stained glass and little stained glass houses. It reminded Daniel of a church.

"Danny, what the heck?" Kevane gasped.

"This is crazy," Daniel said. "I've never seen anything like it. Maybe some thieves are storing their stolen stuff down here. Then we're really in big trouble if they show up."

"No, I don't think so," Kevane said. "Look how everything is displayed. There are outlets in the walls. There used to be electricity in here! I bet lights were supposed to shine on this stuff so it would show off all the colors. I bet anything the guy who brought all this stuff here died. So now it's not doing anybody any good."

"I know where you're going, Kev," Daniel said. "But don't."

"Dan, it's crazy for all this good stuff to be just buried underground," Kevane said in frustration.

"Look, there's another door," Daniel said, suddenly energized with curiosity. "Wonder where that one leads . . ."

They moved carefully through the doorway into another room. It was a library with walnut paneling covering the rock walls. The bookcases had glass doors that rolled open. Some of the books had embossed leather binding with gold trim, but others were just ordinary books.

Daniel went to one case of books and slid open the glass door. "Hey, this book is titled *The Mushroom Cloud: The Damned and the Doomed.* Weird."

"What's a mushroom cloud?" Kevane asked.

"Haven't you heard of a mushroom cloud?" Daniel asked. "Way back in the old days when Grandpa was a kid, the clouds that came from atomic explosions were called *mushroom clouds*. There'd be this big explosion, and then this huge cloud would grow into the sky like a giant white mushroom." Daniel opened the book and looked at the copyright page. It was published in 1958. He flipped through a few pages and said, "It's about the bomb, yeah."

Kevane reached for another book. It was about the atomic bombs dropped at Hiroshima and Nagasaki. He started flipping through it. "Sick. This is full of really gory pictures."

Daniel started plucking down book after book, and he found they were all on the same subject—the atomic bomb. None of them had been published after the early 1960s.

"Maybe the guy who built this place was a terrorist who liked bombs," Kevane said.

Daniel shook his head. "No. I bet this place is a huge underground bomb shelter.

The guy who built it was probably terrified of the atomic bomb, so he built this place and brought all his treasurers here so he could save them when war came. Remember Grandpa telling us about when he was a young boy and everybody was afraid of atomic bombs?"

"Yeah," Kevane said. "He said a lot of people built little bomb shelters in their backyards and stored supplies so they could go down there and hide until the fires were over and the radiation wasn't so strong."

"In 1963, the president came on TV and told everybody that the Third World War might be coming, and then people really started hiding in their shelters or heading for the desert," Daniel said. "Grandpa laughs about it now, but I guess it was pretty serious stuff back then."

"Yeah. The guy who built this place was probably sure everything was going to be destroyed above ground, and so he crawled down here to be safe," Kevane said.

"But then what?" Daniel asked. "The guy must have seen that it wasn't happening like he'd thought. So why didn't he come back up and start living like a human being again instead of like a gopher?"

"Maybe he didn't get the chance," Kevane said. His eyes widened.

"What's that supposed to mean?" Daniel asked. "The war never happened. Nobody dropped atomic bombs on us. The guy had to see it was safe to come up into the world again."

"Maybe he wasn't thinking straight anymore. Maybe he was so scared about the bomb that it made him crazy. Maybe he just hid down here . . ." Kevane said.

"Until what?" Daniel asked.

"Until . . . you know, he died or something," Kevane said.

Daniel laughed nervously. "Oh, yeah, right. Now you're saying he's down here dead, right? Like we're going to open another door and there he'll be, a skeleton in his bathrobe sitting in his chair reading a doomsday book, right? I think your imagination is getting away from you again."

"I have a feeling that the crazy guy is down here somewhere . . ."

The amused look left Daniel's face. "So this is like a cemetery or something?"

"A mausoleum," Kevane said. "Like the pyramids where the famous guys were buried with all their treasures."

Daniel didn't say anything, but he did not have a good feeling about this.

In fact, he was a little scared.

3 "Man," Kevane said, "if Arthur was with us now and he heard us talking about skeletons around the next corner, he'd want to get out of here *fast*!"

"I kinda feel that way too," Daniel admitted.

Kevane laughed. "But, hey, if the guy is dead, he doesn't care if we look around, right? I mean, who's afraid of a dead man? What would he care if we even took a couple of souvenirs?"

"Forget it," Daniel said. "The stuff here would belong to his relatives, not us."

"What if he didn't have any relatives?" Kevane asked. He was already looking at the next door. Daniel could tell he was wondering if something even more awesome was behind it.

The place was built in a strange way. The rooms were connected to one another without a hallway.

"Are you wanting to open that door?" Daniel asked Kevane.

"Maybe he's there," Kevane said.

"You mean the dead guy?" Daniel asked in a brave voice.

"Yeah. If he died down here, he must be somewhere. His bones anyway," Kevane said.

"You sure you're up for seeing a skeleton?" Daniel asked.

"What's the big deal?" Kevane said. "I've seen skeletons before."

"Not real ones. Plastic ones in Halloween houses," Daniel reminded his brother.

"I'm not some scared little kid," Kevane snapped.

The boys approached the door. All of a sudden they heard a strange sound coming from behind it. They stopped and stared at each other. At first it sounded like a low hum, but then it grew louder, turning into a moan.

"Oh, man," Kevane said, "what's *that*?"

"Something behind that door is making the noise," Daniel said. "That's for sure."

The moaning continued. Or maybe it wasn't moaning. Maybe it only *sounded* like moaning. Daniel couldn't be sure.

"Maybe somebody is hurt in there and needs help," Daniel said. "Maybe somebody wandered in here just like we did and fell down or something. Do you think we should look?"

"Yeah," Kevane said, but not very confidently.

Daniel grasped the doorknob and turned it. Both boys trained their flashlights ahead of them. Daniel shouted, "Hello! Anybody here?"

"Look!" Kevane gasped. Daniel turned his eyes to the walls of the room. They were mounted with hundreds of animal heads and birds. Antlered bucks erupted from the walnut-paneled walls. Great hawks hung from iron chains in the ceiling. A full-sized cougar crouched in a grotto cut from the wall. "They look almost alive!"

"It's taxidermy," Daniel said. "Guys mount the skins of animals and birds they've killed like trophies. All these creatures look like they could be from around here. The guy who lived here must have been quite a hunter."

The moaning sound continued. It seemed to come from high up the wall. "I bet it's just the wind," Kevane said. "There's probably a little hole up there in the rocks where the wind gets in."

"Yeah," Daniel said, relaxing a bit, "or maybe some kind of bird makes that sound. Like a dove or an owl. Birds could come and go through openings we can't even see up there."

Daniel walked toward the head of a magnificent buck. "Look at this animal. Those antlers have six points on each side. Seems a shame to kill an animal like that," he said.

"Dan, look at this," Kevane said, shining his flashlight on the floor. It was a crossword puzzle carefully cut from a newspaper.

Kevane stooped and picked up the puzzle. It was mostly done in ink. A few squares were still blank. "It's not yellowed with age," he said. "And listen, one of the questions asks for a five-letter rodent that you click on. A computer mouse, right?"

Daniel frowned. "They didn't have personal computers in the late '50s and early '60s. A mouse in those days was just a furry little rodent. So that means somebody has been here a lot more recently than we'd thought. I just figured the man who built this must have died, but maybe he didn't. Maybe he's still here, but he just stopped collecting books. Let's see, if he was just a young guy in the '50s, he'd have to be in his eighties now, right? That's possible. He might still be holed up here."

Kevane looked alarmed. "You mean he's been hiding down here for 50 years or more? How would a young guy have had the money to build all this? The guy who built this place had to have been a millionaire or something."

"Maybe an older man built it, and his son stayed on," Daniel said.

"No way," Kevane laughed. "No kid is going to hang down here for very long."

Daniel walked to the head of the buck again. He had not noticed the bronze plate before, but now he read the inscription. "Taken in the hunt by Ernest Abbott Overton, November 1938."

"That must be the guy who built this place," Kevane said. "Even his name sounds rich, doesn't it?"

Daniel laughed. He knew his parents were doing well, but they were far from rich. His dad worked in insurance, and his mom was an accountant. They owned a nice home and didn't have to struggle to get what the family needed, but they would never be rich. Whoever excavated the mountain to build this underground world and fill it with rich treasures must have been incredibly wealthy.

"I bet there's another entrance to this place," Daniel said. "That trapdoor we came in hadn't been used in a while. You know—" Daniel broke off when the moaning sounds returned louder than before.

The sound was filled with distress. It seemed to be coming directly from the red-tailed hawk suspended in air above them. It began to sound like a human voice crying in pain.

"What is that?" Kevane cried. "It sounds like somebody dying or something!"

"Maybe some hiker came down here and got stuck," Daniel said. "Maybe he's the guy who dropped the crossword puzzle. He might've fallen into a crevice and broken his leg or something. Or . . . or maybe whoever lives down here got ahold of the poor guy, and he's in some dungeon . . ." All kinds of possible horrors rushed through Daniel's mind. Maybe there was some monster living down here.

"We've gotta get out of here!" Kevane shouted.

"Yeah, you're right," Daniel said. "Maybe somebody needs help, but the best thing we can do for him is to get out of here fast and call the police. If we stick around much longer, then whoever got him will get us too."

"Right," Kevane said.

They backtracked, going through the library again. Daniel threw his flashlight beam across the books and noticed titles he had not seen before.

Chamber of Doom: The World on Fire was one title. On the spine of another book was written *The Ashen Tomb*. And then Daniel saw the huge painting, all red and white and black. He had paid no attention to the wild mixture of colors before, but now when he glanced at it, he could see faces in the flames—twisted, deformed, pain-filled faces, their mouths gaping in shock and horror.

"Look at that!" Daniel gasped.

"Looks like something a crazy person painted," Kevane said. "Come on, hurry. We've gotta get up to that trapdoor."

Daniel glimpsed the name scrawled at the bottom of the painting. "Overton."

Ernest Abbott Overton had painted the horrific scene—the same guy who shot the buck and had its head mounted on the wall. He was probably some dangerous recluse. Maybe he was still here, Daniel thought. Maybe he was lurking in the middle of this underground world like a deadly spider lurks in the center of her web waiting for victims. Maybe Overton had a kind of web too, and if you tripped it, you were gone. Maybe that poor guy who was groaning had tripped a wire in the web.

The boys hurried into the stained glass room and rushed toward the other door. This was the last door before they were in the coconut room, and then the small outer room, and finally up the stairs to the trapdoor.

"What do we do first when we're out of here?" Kevane asked, his voice coming in breathless gasps from running and talking at the same time.

"Run as fast as we can back to camp and call the police on Dad's cell phone," Daniel said. "Hope they get here in time if that is some poor guy in trouble."

The stained glass, even in the darkness, dazzled them with its beauty. But neither boy spent any time looking at it as they hurried to the door. Daniel reached it first and grasped the doorknob. "What the—!" he cried.

"What's the matter?" Kevane demanded. "Open it! Turn the knob. Quit messing around!"

"I'm not messing around!" Daniel said grimly. "The stupid door won't open. It's locked or something!"

"It can't be locked!" Kevane cried. "We just came through there!" Kevane pushed past his older brother and grasped the doorknob himself, trying to turn it. "Man, this isn't happening! How could this be happening! We just got through here less than an hour ago!"

"Maybe it's a self-locking door," Daniel groaned. "Maybe that's one of the security tricks the guy put in so he'd slow down anybody coming through . . ." Daniel looked up and down the door. It was solid oak. It wasn't like those cheap, new plywood doors in many houses today. You could bust through those doors. But this door was solid. "I don't know how we're gonna get out of here, Kev . . ."

"We've gotta get out," Kevane said. "Listen, something awful is going on down here, and if it finds us, we're done for. You hear what I'm saying?" Kevane was stunned and frightened. "We're in big trouble if we don't get out of here . . ."

"Take it easy," Daniel said. "Don't panic." But deep in his own heart that's just where he was going.

Panic City.

4 Daniel kept trying the door. It wasn't budging, but he didn't know what else to do. Finally, frustrated, he turned to his brother.

"You know what?" he said harshly. "Maybe Mom and Dad are gonna need Arthur now to have a kid in the house. Maybe your stupid curiosity is gonna cost us our necks!"

Kevane turned sharply. "Hey, I feel bad enough," he said in an agonized voice. "Do you have to make me feel worse?"

Daniel regretted what he'd said. He was just so angry at himself for letting Kevane talk him into coming into this trap. He was the older brother. He should have known better.

"Okay, okay, we've got to figure a way out of here," Daniel said. "We've got to escape. Obviously we can't go back the way we came in, so we've got to keep going deeper into the place so we can find the other entrance. There has to be another entrance."

Kevane seemed to brighten a little. "Yeah, yeah, maybe the other entrance is real close, like just beyond the room with the stuffed animal heads," he said.

The boys turned and retraced their steps to the library. Daniel pushed desperate thoughts from his mind. He was afraid the library door would now be locked, and they'd be trapped right where they were. When they reached the door, he took a deep breath. When he grasped the doorknob, the door opened. Daniel began to relax a little. Maybe the locked door to the coconut head room was just an accident. Maybe it had slammed shut in a draft and locked automatically. Maybe there wasn't some evil madman in the center of this web orchestrating the whole thing, deliberately keeping the boys from escaping.

Maybe even the terrible groaning sounds could be explained naturally. Maybe birds or the wind *was* causing the sounds, and the guys' imaginations had filled in the rest.

Maybe there was nothing sinister about this place after all.

They reached the taxidermy room and then spotted a door at the other side where they had not yet been. Daniel stopped for a moment, staring at it. He didn't hear any more moaning sounds. Maybe the doves—or whatever was making the noise—had gone away. "Well, Kev, looks like we'd better just open that door and see what's on the other side, right?" Daniel asked in a brave voice, covering the queasy feelings inside.

"Yeah, open it," Kevane said nervously.

When Daniel swung the door open and they threw their flashlight beams into the room, they suddenly realized the room was already aglow with dull light. They were looking at a pleasant living room with overstuffed chairs and leather recliners. There were walnut end tables and lamps. Most amazing of all, the lamps glowed faintly.

"It's impossible," Kevane gasped. "There couldn't be electricity down here . . ."

"Must be a generator," Daniel said. He led the way into a hallway that went into a bedroom and bathroom. "This is where he must live, or where he lived . . . I bet the other entrance is right around here."

The bedroom was dark, but with their flashlights, the boys illuminated a large poster bed and an old-fashioned, tall dresser with a beautiful mirror that had oak-leaf clusters carved on the frame. "Looks pretty neat and clean," Kevane said.

Daniel went into the bathroom. He could hardly believe his eyes. It looked just like any other bathroom. He turned on the water faucet in the sink, and to his shock, water flowed out! "Man! He must have been one smart guy to even get water to this place. You think it's from a well?" he asked.

"Maybe a mountain spring," Kevane said. "The guy was some kind of genius all right to put all this together in the middle of nowhere. Where do you think the exit is?"

"I thought I saw a kitchen off the hall," Daniel replied. "Maybe we can get out from there."

The kitchen had an old refrigerator and stove. Kevane stared at the refrigerator for a few minutes. Surely it couldn't be working. But then the lights worked, even though they only cast a faint glow.

Kevane gingerly pulled open the refrigerator door, and a light came on inside! "Hey, Danny, there's stuff in here. Hot dogs, orange juice, milk!" he yelled.

Daniel hurried to his brother's side. "It's all from a generator. The guy must have figured when the war came and the bombs started flying, the utilities would all stop and he'd need his own power source," he said. "But you know what all this means, don't you? Somebody is living here right now. We're in somebody's home. We could get busted for breaking and entering!"

"But we don't *want* to be here," Kevane said. "We want to get out. It's not our fault."

"It's not that easy," Daniel said. "Nobody invited us to open that door, come down those stairs, and then go from room to room snooping around. If we saw a neighbor's door standing open, would we just walk in and start looking at his stuff? We're burglars, man!"

"No, we're not," Kevane argued. "We just got curious. Anybody else would've done the same thing."

"Yeah, and if I hadn't stopped you, you would have ripped off one of those coconut heads with the jewel eyes," Daniel said. "So then we'd be thieves too."

Kevane remembered the little dove he had plucked and stuck in his shirt pocket. He felt for it. It was still there. He had meant to take it out at camp before the barbecue, but he was so into his dad's steaks that he had forgotten all about it.

"Look, you're just as much to blame as me for all of this," Kevane growled. "You were curious too. You didn't have to come in. I probably wouldn't have come down alone. How come you didn't turn around and head back to camp? I would have followed you. I would've been mad, but I would've followed you."

The boys heard a crackling sound then, the kind of noise they would hear at Cleveland High School just before Mr. Webb, the principal, was about to make an important announcement over the intercom.

A trembling voice boomed into the kitchen where Daniel and Kevane stood.

"You vile scoundrels, you have invaded the privacy of my home," the voice accused.

"Oh, great!" Kevane groaned.

Daniel thought it sounded like the voice of an 80-year-old man. Maybe it was Ernest Abbott Overton himself.

"Let me handle this," Daniel said. "Uh, Mr. Overton? We're real sorry. It was all a big mistake. We came to this trapdoor, and we thought it was just a hole in the ground. Then we got curious, and we kept getting in deeper and deeper. We thought this place was abandoned, or we never would've come in."

"Yeah," Kevane chimed in, "and we'd be long gone except we couldn't get out the door between the stained glass room and the place where the coconut heads are. If you'd just open that door, we'll be gone in two seconds."

The strange voice came again. "You have invaded my home. You have violated my privacy. You will bring others, and my solitude will be destroyed."

"No, see, we won't tell anyone about this," Daniel promised. "Our parents are camping in the mountains a few miles from here. We'll be going home soon, and we'll forget all about this place. Honest!"

"You have violated my property," the ancient voice crackled. "You have discovered my secret, and you will betray me to the world."

"No, no," Kevane groaned, "we won't tell a soul. Just open that door, and we'll be gone. You'll never hear from us or anybody else again because we'll keep our mouths shut."

Daniel wondered where the man's voice was coming from. He thought they had been through all the rooms, but apparently there was yet another room where this man was holed up. "Look, Mr. Overton, just open the door, and we're out of your hair, okay?" Daniel pleaded.

"There is no escape from here. Whoever comes to this place never returns to the world," the strange voice bellowed. "Never, never, never . . ."

There was some static, then, briefly, the terrible sounds of groaning again, and then silence.

"You know," Daniel whispered, "I don't think we were talking to anybody. I think that was a recorded message. The groans too. I think the guy put in a sound system to scare intruders away. He probably recorded that message 40 years ago!"

"But he was talking to us," Kevane said. "He was answering what we were saying!"

"No, he wasn't," Daniel argued. "He just kept saying the same stuff over and over. And those groaning sounds shut off real fast, like a cassette or a CD stopped playing."

"But someone's here!" Kevane insisted. "Someone locked the door on us. Someone started talking to us, or at least played the message."

"Come on, let's get out of this part of the house. Maybe whoever's here can watch us better from the living quarters," Daniel said, grabbing his brother's arm.

The boys ran back to the taxidermy room.

"This place is so spooky," Kevane said. "It's like those creepy animals are staring at us with their glass eyes!"

"Okay, we'll go to the library," Daniel said, suddenly feeling like the brave one.

They walked into the library. Daniel shone his flashlight on the bookshelves again.

"You know," Kevane said, "maybe there's a secret exit behind the bookshelves. In the movies, there's always an escape hatch behind the books."

"They're just stupid, old books," Daniel said. "There's no exit."

Daniel noticed that not all the books on the shelves were about death and destruction. There were photo albums too. He took one of them down and opened it, illuminating the pages with the beam of his flashlight. "Look," he said, "here's snapshots of Overton hunting. See the skinny old guy with the hunting rifle and one foot on a dead animal?"

Kevane leaned closer for a look. "The pictures are dated. They're from the 1930s. And he looks like an old man already! How could he still be alive in this house?"

Daniel flipped a few more pages. There were dozens of snapshots of the man hunting in the mountains that resembled the area around them. There were no pictures of anyone else—just the old man displaying dead game or walking on a lonely trail.

"He's a regular egomaniac," Daniel said. "Nobody but him in the pictures. And look, these pictures were taken before Grandpa was born!"

Kevane turned on his flashlight and held it by a large picture showing the lined face of Mr. Overton. "He has to be at least 60 here."

"He couldn't be," Daniel said. "That'd make him around 130 or so now."

Kevane's eyes turned wild in the faint light. "Maybe he's a mad scientist, Dan. Maybe he's found the secret to living way past when people are supposed to die. I read on the Internet that people could live to be 150 maybe, that scientists are working on that. Maybe this old guy has the secret. He's a fossil, but he's still alive! Maybe living down here in this weird, cold place is good for him. Maybe it's like when turtles hibernate or something," Kevane said.

"That's just stupid," Daniel said with a shrug.

"*You* figure it," Kevane snapped. "The pictures are labeled 'Captain Overton gets his game.' So it's him, all right. And he's old. He was old way back when. And now he's down here, somehow still alive, and he's holding all the cards. We're like pawns in his hands . . ."

"There's got to be a reasonable explanation," Daniel insisted.

"No, we're goners. The madman is in charge," Kevane said in despair.

"Hey, look," Daniel said, excitement in his voice. "There's a row of buttons right here behind the photo albums. You think one of them might roll back a door?"

Kevane stared at the buttons. "I bet it's a trap. If you push any of those buttons, the room will probably fill up with some kind of gas. Or maybe the ceiling will open up and a swarm of bats will come down on us. It's a trick the old madman has rigged, I'm telling you," he said.

"I don't think so," Daniel said. "I think this is some kind of system connected to the books . . . Like maybe there's another room full of books behind this one."

"Come on, don't touch the buttons!" Kevane pleaded.

"Look, little brother, we can't cower in fear or we'll never get out," Daniel said, his finger poised over the first button in the row.

5 "Danny, don't," Kevane almost screamed.

"Don't be a psycho, Kevane," Daniel said. "There aren't any bats waiting to swoop down on us." But Daniel was nervous too. He didn't expect a swarm of bats, but he wouldn't have been surprised if the floor beneath them gave way.

But he had no choice.

Daniel pushed the button firmly and then heard a creaking sound. Both boys looked up to see a trapdoor in the ceiling roll back. With much wheezing and clanging, a steel ladder fell slowly down until it was firmly planted in the middle of the floor.

"Wow . . . what do you think is up there?" Daniel gasped.

"Let's find out," Kevane said, mounting the ladder first. Daniel followed.

At the top of the ladder, the boys saw a cave. The walls were natural rock.

"What do you think this was used for?" Kevane asked after he scrambled from the ladder onto the floor of the high cave.

"Maybe a wine cellar," Daniel said, but he didn't see any bottles of wine lying around.

When the boys threw their flashlight beams on the walls, they saw beautiful colors—greens and lavenders from the minerals in the rock.

"Maybe this was the last-ditch bomb shelter," Daniel said. "Maybe he figured that if his underground house got contaminated by the radiation, he could find refuge here. It's kind of pathetic to think of a man so scared that he'd go to these extremes."

"Look, this is sort of like a tunnel," Kevane said. "See how it goes farther over there, like a mine shaft."

"Hey, maybe this is the exit we were looking for," Daniel said. "Maybe if we follow the tunnel, it'll lead us out of here. If we get out in the mountains, we'll be able to find our way back to camp. We've got a compass."

"You think there really is an exit at the end of this tunnel?" Kevane asked, his hopes rising. "Man, I'll be so glad to get out of here."

They moved carefully along the slippery rocks, lighting the path ahead with their flashlight beams.

"It's damp in here. That probably means rainwater gets in. Maybe there's an opening somewhere," Daniel said.

They crawled silently for a few minutes longer.

"I see light up ahead!" Kevane suddenly shouted.

"Yeah, yeah, I see it too," Daniel said. "The sun's about going down, and we're looking at the last rays. Wow, we're getting out of here just in time."

The tunnel widened, and suddenly they were in a larger room. High up in the ceiling there was a crack no wider than Daniel's little finger. The fading sunlight was filtering down through the crack.

Disappointment stabbed Daniel. He had expected to find a great, gaping hole inviting their escape. But there was only a crack, a tantalizing reminder of the outside world of freedom—nothing more. He felt like a condemned prisoner staring through iron bars. They were as trapped as ever in this strange world.

"Why couldn't that crack be bigger?" Kevane said, sounding nearly defeated. "Man, nothing but a lizard could get through that."

Daniel spotted it then, the box in the corner of the cave. "What's that?" he said aloud.

Kevane turned and stared at the long, narrow box too. It was covered with a beautiful cloth that looked like velvet. There was no dust near the box, suggesting that someone was taking care of it. A stained glass angel, supported by a wooden base, stood atop the box. It glowed in an eerie way, seeming to catch the light perfectly from the crack in the ceiling.

"It's, uh . . . it's an angel," Kevane said. "Somebody, uh . . . put an angel on top of that box . . ."

"Yeah," Daniel said matter-of-factly. "Looks like."

Kevane stood there for another minute not saying a word. Then he said in a very low voice, "Why would somebody put an angel on top of a box like that, Dan?"

Daniel shrugged. He sort of knew the answer. Kevane did too. But neither of them wanted to come right out and say what was on his mind. "People do strange things, Kev. Come on, we'd better go back. There's no way out of here."

Kevane threw his flashlight beam around again, making sure. "Yeah. The tunnel ends here. This is it. The trapdoor just led to this high cave and nothing else . . ." he said.

"You know, even if this isn't a way out, maybe we ought to hide here," Daniel suggested. "I pulled up the ladder and closed the door, so the guy probably doesn't know we're up here. If we hide here for a while, maybe he'll think we got out somehow, and he'll forget about us. Then maybe he'll get careless and open the door between the stained glass room and the room with the coconut heads."

Kevane glanced over at the box with the angel on top. "What do you think's in that box?" he asked in a dread-filled voice.

"Nothing that can hurt us," Daniel

answered evasively. "Stop thinking about it, okay?"

"Why would somebody put an angel on top of a long, narrow box like that?" Kevane demanded. He walked slowly over and trained his flashlight on the angel for a moment. It glittered in the light.

"Kevane!" Daniel pleaded.

Kevane ignored his brother. "There's something written here on the rock next to the box. Looks like somebody carved letters in the rock," he said.

"So what?" Daniel said. "Come on, Kev. Just forget about it, okay? Let's just sit tight until night comes. Then maybe we can sneak out of here."

" 'R.I.P.,' " Kevane read. "That's what they write on gravestones. That means the box is a coffin. This cave is like a tomb. Old Overton must be in the box."

"Think about it," Daniel said. "Nobody was down here but him. You think he buried himself?"

"No, somebody else was here," Kevane said. "Remember the crossword puzzle? Some guy stumbled in here, and maybe he and Overton struggled. And Overton lost.

Or maybe the other guy did, huh? Maybe some poor guy who just stumbled in here like we did is in that box. How do you explain that voice saying that nobody who comes in here ever gets out again?"

"Kevane, just leave the box alone," Daniel said, his brain too full to think anymore. "Let's wait until dark, and then we can try to sneak out of here. The guy— whoever he is—has to sleep sometime, right?" In his own heart, he wasn't so sure it would be that easy, but he wanted to get Kevane's mind off the box.

"I don't want to stay in this cave with a dead guy," Kevane said.

"Okay, we could go back to the library if you want, but he's got a better chance of finding us there," Daniel said.

"I feel weird with 'him' over there," Kevane mumbled.

"You don't even know if there *is* a dead guy in the box," Daniel said. "It could just be somebody's idea of a bad joke. You're letting your wild imagination run away with you again. Man, you're such a baby. You're worse than Arthur would be if he was with us. He'd be more grown-up than you are."

Usually remarks like that would set Kevane off, but right now he was too scared even to be offended by his brother's insults. "You know what, Dan? I wouldn't even mind Arthur being with us if I could be back at camp and we were out of here . . . Do you think if I prayed that we get out of here and promised I wouldn't be against Arthur living with us, that'd help or something?"

"You want to make a deal? Us out of here for letting the kid join the family," Daniel said.

"Yeah. What's wrong with that?" Kevane said. "When I was a little kid, I promised I'd stop calling Lawrence Fisher 'hogpants' if I got the bike I wanted. It worked too. I got my bike that Christmas."

"Did you stop calling Lawrence Fisher 'hogpants'?" Daniel asked.

"Sorta," Kevane admitted, "but I still picked on him."

Daniel suddenly realized how tired he was. He leaned on the wall of the cave. After a few minutes he nodded off. He didn't see Kevane get up and walk over to the box again. He didn't see him carefully lift the velvet cover and try to open the box. But as the lid creaked under Kevane's hands, Daniel woke up with a start.

"Kevane, don't," Daniel yelled. He leaped to his feet and ran to his brother's side. He was going to grab Kevane and drag him away from the box before he got it open. "Are you crazy? What do you want to look in there for? What's it going to get you?"

"I gotta know," Kevane said in a flat voice.

Daniel gave up. His arms dropped to his sides and he waited. Kevane couldn't get the lid up because it was nailed down, but when he fiddled with his knife, he found a weak place and began to pry up the plywood. Then Kevane threw his flashlight beam into the open box. Daniel looked too. Neither boy said anything for the first few seconds. Finally Daniel said very softly, "Close it up. Put the cloth back over it and the angel too. We had no right to do what we just did."

Kevane pushed the plywood lid down and pulled the cloth over the box the way it was when they first saw it. His hands were shaking so badly he almost dropped the angel before he could set it back in place.

Then Kevane said, "It must have happened years and years ago, huh?"

"Yeah. Just bones. He's been there a long time," Daniel said.

"Must be Overton," Kevane said. "He probably died in the '60s or something. That's why there aren't any books dated after the early '60s. Because he was dead. But somebody must have buried him. Somebody must have put him in the box and put the cloth over it like that and even set the angel there . . . Maybe his son, you think? His son would be an old man now too, right? The voice that was yelling at us sounded like an old man's . . ."

"Nah," Daniel disagreed. "It doesn't make sense. Maybe the old guy was so scared of the atomic bomb that he came here and holed up until he died, but his son wouldn't have stayed. Had to have been somebody else who buried him."

Kevane glanced up at the moonlight pouring through the crack overhead. "Let's get out of here, okay? I don't want to be here anymore . . ."

"Yeah," Daniel said, glancing at his watch. "It's night. Whoever is down there probably went to bed. If we have any chance of sneaking out of here, now's our best shot."

"You know what?" Kevane said as they scrambled up and strapped on their backpacks. "We've been missing from camp a long time, since early afternoon. Mom and Dad must be really worried. I bet they've called the cops. A whole bunch of people are probably searching for us right now."

"Sure, yeah, but it's a big wilderness area. They don't know what direction we went. Remember that big lake we saw when we drove in? They might think we went for a swim and drowned. They're probably dragging the lake for us," Daniel said.

The boys returned to the first room they had climbed into. A button behind the bookcase in the library had opened the trapdoor and lowered the ladder for them to climb. But when Daniel closed it, he did it manually. There was no button on this side. Now he knelt on the floor and tried to open the trapdoor so he could push the ladder down.

"Come on, come on," Daniel growled at the door. It seemed stuck. "Kevane, come here and help me get this thing up."

Kevane knelt at the other side of the door and tried to pry the door up. His eyes turned wild. "Danny, it won't come up. We're trapped up here in the cave! We'll never get out of here, and we'll turn into a pile of bones like the guy in the box!" Kevane groaned.

Daniel felt his own mouth go dry, but he didn't show his fear to Kevane. "Come on, man, help me pry it up. *Come on!* We can do it!"

6 Daniel stuck his knife in the crack and pried, and this time he felt the door yield a little. "It's coming! Help me, Kev . . . We can get it up."

Little by little they got their fingers under the door and raised it. Then they dropped the ladder and went scampering down the steps to the library.

"We've gotta be real quiet," Daniel cautioned. "If there is someone down here, we want him to keep out of our way."

"What do you mean 'if'?" Kevane whispered. "There's gotta be someone down here. Remember that voice that talked to us? And how did the door between the stained glass room and the coconut head room lock on us? Somebody is masterminding all this."

"Maybe not. Maybe Mr. Overton rigged up a lot of automatic things. Maybe he wasn't only afraid of the bomb. Maybe he was afraid of intruders too. Maybe everything that's happened is just automatic from a system he put in ages ago. You know what, Kevane? Maybe we're being terrorized by a bunch of cassette tapes in machines!" Daniel said.

"Come on," Kevane argued, "the lights still work in the kitchen, and there's stuff in the fridge!"

"Okay, I'll give you that. From time to time people have been down here. But maybe they were just guys like us who came and went. Maybe there's nobody here *now*," Daniel said.

"Well, anyway, let's move," Kevane said.

The boys hurried from the library and went into the stained glass room. Daniel hoped the door leading to the room with the coconut heads would be open this time. If some automatic system locked it, maybe it automatically came open again. Daniel was dreading grasping the doorknob and discovering they were still trapped, but he had to find out.

"Okay, here goes nothing," Daniel said, grasping the knob firmly.

He twisted it, but it would not open.

"Oh, great," Kevane groaned. "I have a bad feeling that somebody is watching us. I feel like a rat in a science-lab experiment. Some madman is watching us race around trying to get out, and he knows it's hopeless. Just like the scientist knows the poor rat won't ever escape the maze."

"Just shut up for a minute!" Daniel snapped. He studied the door frame looking for some way to get through, but it was strong and firm. Using his knife, he tried to pick the lock, but that didn't work either.

Then, suddenly, as the boys stood at the door, a strange voice spoke from the darkness behind them, "The door is jammed. It won't open. I cannot imagine why. It does that sometimes."

Kevane grabbed his brother's arm for support, and they both turned to see a dark figure standing in front of one of the stained glass windows. At first he looked like a ghost. Daniel felt sick to his stomach. He figured he was actually face-to-face with some dark spirit from another world.

But when the boys shone their flashlight beams at the figure, they could clearly see that it was a man. He was of medium height and build, with long, flowing gray-white hair like a wizard. He was dressed in black trousers and a black overcoat, and his face was wrinkled and lined. It was a gray color, as if he was very old, perhaps older than anyone they had ever seen before. But his eyes were very bright, like a hawk's eyes, and they sparkled almost as much as the stained glass.

"Who are you?" Daniel asked. Kevane was so scared that he had momentarily lost his voice, so he couldn't say anything. All he could do was stare at the man and wonder if this was indeed Ernest Abbott Overton, well past his hundredth year.

"I might ask you the same question," the quivering old voice asked. "And in courtesy, you ought to answer me first because you are intruders in my home."

"I'm Daniel Robinson and this is my brother, Kevane. Our folks are camped a few miles from here, and we just stumbled in here by mistake. We're really sorry. We saw the trapdoor, and we just thought this was an abandoned mine or something. We didn't mean to bust into somebody's house. We're really sorry. All we want to do now is get out of here," Daniel said.

"But there is no escape," the man said, though not in a hostile voice. He sounded almost sad. "You can enter, but you can't get out, you see."

"No, no," Daniel argued. "Just a few hours ago we got through this door. Now it's locked. You could open it, right?"

"No, I have forgotten all the controls in this place," the man explained. "Now things just happen you see, willy-nilly, and it's as much a surprise to me as to anyone else. I built this shelter as a refuge from the madness of thermonuclear war in 1952. I was a highly paid engineer in those days, and I understood the danger the world was facing, the destruction of all human and animal life from the planet earth by the forces of evil hatred. But now I am old, and my mind has forgotten all the technicalities that I once understood."

Daniel and Kevane looked at each other in disbelief. Finally Daniel asked the man, "Are you Mr. Overton?"

"Oh, indeed. Ernest Abbott Overton," he said with a distinct note of pride. "I was a world traveler in my time, a big game hunter, the respected designer of skyscrapers and bridges."

"But you'd have to be over a hundred years old!" Kevane finally found the voice to say. "We saw pictures of you from the 1930s, and you looked like an old—I mean, you weren't a kid!"

The bright eyes, the only youthful feature on the ancient face, sparkled from the gray mask of wrinkles. The man looked right at Kevane and said, "I may have looked old in those photographs, but I was a youth. I have always looked older than my years. My mother used to tell me I was an old-looking child even. So, you see, I am not yet 100 years old now, but I am close to it, I must confess."

Kevane looked wildly at Daniel. Daniel could tell Kevane wasn't thinking straight. It was all too scary, too horrible, so he blurted out what was on his mind. "You're

dead, man! I saw your bones in the box in
the cave. You're dead!"

The man laughed in a crackly voice,
almost chuckled. "Ah, no, no. The body in
the coffin is that of a stranger. A young
fellow much like you two. He came down
uninvited to visit me, and he roamed
around for a while, finding he could not
escape. He went in circles, growing more
desperate all the while, until he tried in
desperation to crawl out a small crevice in
the ceiling and fell to his death. Of course
I had to give him a decent burial, poor
wretch. And he was a thief too, as you
are."

"We're not thieves," Daniel snapped.
"We didn't take anything."

"Ah, you walked through the room
where the coconut carvings have diamond
and ruby eyes, and you did not snatch
even one lovely item for yourself?" the
man demanded.

"No," Daniel cried indignantly. Kevane
felt his face growing uncomfortably
warm. The dove with the ruby eyes was
still in his top shirt pocket. Even though it
was very small, right then it felt like it

created a huge bulge for all to see.

"Every man is a thief if given the opportunity," the man argued. "The corruption of mankind drove me to this refuge, and as sure as I stand here, you are thieves."

"That's a lie," Daniel said in a righteous voice.

The man finally drew away from the stained-glass window he leaned against. He walked with an amazingly brisk stride for someone who admitted to being almost 100 years old. Daniel's grandparents were in their late sixties, and even they had slowed down a bit. "I shall prove to you that you are thieves," the man said, drawing a small talisman from his shirt. "This is a most amazing object. If I point it at a person and he has in his possession one of the carvings with jewel eyes, the object he conceals will immediately burst into flames with such an intense fire that it cannot be extinguished until the hapless thief is a pillar of ash. Now then, shall I aim my talisman at you, or will you voluntarily turn over the object you have stolen?"

Daniel didn't believe in the power of the talisman for a minute. It was a bluff. But he also had a clear conscience, so he said, "Aim anything you want at me. I didn't take anything."

Kevane didn't really believe in the power of the talisman either, but he wasn't willing to take a chance. So he pulled the dove from his pocket and said, "I just borrowed this thing to look at it, but I was going to put it back before we left!"

"Aha!" the man crowed. "I knew it. I knew it."

Daniel glared at his brother. His narrowed eyes demanded, "How could you do that, you little jerk?"

"It's not anything," Kevane cried. "It's just a stupid little piece of junk. I didn't think it belonged to anybody. It was like taking a pinecone from the woods or something."

"Thief!" the man continued to crow. "And to take a pinecone from the woods is thievery too, for it is a seed for the next generation of pine trees."

"Look," Daniel said, "I'm sorry my idiot brother took the dove. I'm really sorry.

He's just a stupid kid." As Daniel drew nearer to the man, the man backed away. He seemed more comfortable with distance between them. He shrank into the glow of the stained glass works.

"Mr. Overton, we just want to get out of here and go back to our parents," Daniel explained. "Surely there's a way out."

"No, there isn't one that I know of," he said.

"But when we were in the kitchen, we opened the fridge, and there was food in there. There was fresh orange juice and hot dogs. I mean, you must go in and out to get supplies," Daniel said.

"You were even spying on my personal things," the man shrieked. He had a strange, nasal voice. He was a little hoarse too, but Daniel was beginning to notice that sometimes he didn't sound as old as he did other times. It was almost as if he was faking his voice.

"I'm sorry, Mr. Overton," Daniel said, "but we were just looking for a way out of here."

"Whoever comes to this place never returns to the world," the ancient voice declared. "I have many supplies in my cupboard. I prepared for a long period of isolation as the deadly radiation covered the earth from the nuclear war. I believed I would be one of only a few left, and it would be up to us to begin again the human race. So I stocked up on everything. Come, I will show you." He led the way back to the kitchen and opened cupboard doors where cans and boxes were stacked. There was dried milk, powdered orange juice, most everything. But Daniel noted in his own mind that there were no hot dogs. "You see?" the man said, "I have no need to leave here to get new supplies."

"You know," Daniel said carefully, "if we were to get out of here, we wouldn't tell anybody about this place. I swear we'd keep it a secret."

The man made a cackling laugh. "Indeed! You would not keep quiet for a moment. They would come here by the hordes to see the freak living in the underground house. They would parade me before television cameras. They would put me away in a hospital for the insane."

"No, honest, we wouldn't," Daniel said.

The man seemed to soften a little. He was quiet for a few moments. Then he said, "You are welcome to share my supplies. There is plenty of food here. I have instant soups and powdered potatoes. Meats, instant coffee. I have a pure water supply, you know. He was a genius. He provided for everything. The generator, everything. It's a world within a world," he said.

Daniel glanced at Kevane. He wondered if his brother had caught the slip in the man's words too. The man had said 'he was a genius.' He had spoken in the third person, as if he were talking about somebody else. Just for a moment he tipped his hand.

So this was *not* Ernest Abbott Overton. It was somebody else—someone who had moved into this world and claimed a new identity. But Daniel decided not to admit what he had heard. It might only make matters worse. It might put the man on the defensive, and he was probably dangerous. Daniel decided a better way would be to try to win his confidence, slowly work on him and get him to show them a way out of here. He had to know a way out. He must have gotten those hot dogs recently.

"Well, I guess some orange juice would be pretty good right now," Daniel said.

"Help yourself," the man said.

Daniel poured two cups of orange juice from the bottle in the refrigerator. They sat down at a table in the kitchen.

"I must take care of something now," the man said, excusing himself. He moved quickly off. Then he turned and said, as if in afterthought, "Oh, my. When I forget myself and move too quickly, my old joints remind me of my many years." With that he limped off.

"He's a fake," Daniel whispered to his brother.

"Yeah, he talked about Overton being a genius," Kevane said. "So he's not Overton. This freak probably came along and killed the old man. Then he stuck him in that box. This guy's probably a criminal."

"I don't think so," Daniel whispered back. "If he was a criminal, he would have found a way to haul all this valuable stuff out of here and sell it. There must be a fortune down here in stained glass alone. He'd be spending the money and enjoying life. No, I think he's a weirdo of some kind . . . to be living down here in this *tomb*!"

"Yeah," Kevane agreed. "I wonder what he really looks like. That gray face and all those wrinkles. He looks like he's made up for Halloween or something. Mr. Dudley on our street is in his nineties, and he doesn't look like that."

"Must be makeup," Daniel said. "When he heard us moving around, he probably made himself up to look like he thought Overton would look. He probably uses makeup when he goes shopping too."

"Danny," Kevane asked, "do you think he'll change his mind and let us out, or are we stuck here forever?"

"We've got to get him to trust us. Maybe we could agree with the stuff in those library books, make him think he did a great thing hiding down here and preserving all those treasures in case the world got blown up," Daniel said.

"You know," Kevane said, "this is really good orange juice. I can't believe it came from some old powder."

"Yeah, it tastes fresh," Daniel agreed. "I'm sure he got it recently too."

The boys began wandering around the underground place, checking out the stained glass room, then ending up in the library, all the while looking over their shoulders for the strange man. In the library, they took down some more of the photo albums. There were photos of Mr. Overton with his colleagues at an engineering firm in Los Angeles. There were even photos of him as a child and teenager. Then Daniel found a wedding album.

"Wow, here he was getting married in the 1920s," Daniel said. "Look at the bride. She was really pretty. She looked like a movie star."

Kevane looked over Daniel's shoulder. "I wonder if they had kids," he said.

The voice of the man crackled behind them then. "I see you discovered the story of my life. Ah, I have had a very full life, eh? Did you see the lovely girl I married?

Her name was Lillian Amsterdam. We had a splendid time. Honeymooned in Paris. Thirty grand years . . . yes, indeed . . ."

Daniel decided to go along with the farce. If the guy, whoever he was, was convinced that the boys believed him, then he might not feel threatened by them. He might let them go. "Did you, uh . . . have children, Mr. Overton?" Daniel asked.

"No, no children, but a wonderful, full life. Lillian played the violin. Her instrument is in the stained glass room. She played like an angel. We had 30 years together. Thirty years of love and fulfillment. What a great love story. The photographs are all there to prove it. And the diaries too. There are 12 diaries, and I've read them all. Jaunts to Europe. Holidays in the Swiss Alps . . ." he said. His voice faltered a little, but then he went on in a stronger tone, as if he was forgetting for the moment that he was a very old man. "Not everyone has such a life. Some people have no life at all."

"Yeah, that's true," Daniel said. "Well, you can be proud that you accomplished so much. And, uh . . . it's good that you built this place so you could protect all those treasures in case, you know, atomic war breaks out. My brother and I think it's a real good idea that you've got this place here just in case, you know, anything happens. That's why when we go on our way, we wouldn't tell a soul about what we saw here."

"Yeah," Kevane chimed in. "We really think you're a great guy to be down here protecting all this stuff, like the stained glass and the carvings. You're, uh . . . doing a big service to humanity. It's real important that you can stay and take care of business here, so we'll keep your secret."

The cackling laugh returned. "Who do you think you're fooling?" the man demanded. "You think I'm as crazy as a bat and you can't wait to get out of here and tell the first cop you meet to send the SWAT team down here after me. You'll blow the whistle on me quicker than you can click a mouse!"

Daniel felt a chill go down his spine. If he had any doubt left that this was a much younger man masquerading as Ernest Abbott Overton, that doubt was gone now. This guy knew about SWAT teams and computers. He was savvy to modern things.

"Look," Daniel said in a limp voice, "I really mean what I say. It's good that you're protecting this stuff from destruction."

"Put a cork in it," the man snapped, turning and stomping out, not even pretending to hobble.

7 Daniel and Kevane were alone in the library now. "There has to be a way out of here," Daniel said with new determination. "Let's try the stained glass room."

The boys went into the next room, and Kevane swept his flashlight beam around, finally scanning the ceiling. "What's that square thing?" he asked.

"Hey, I never saw that before. Maybe it's the other exit," Daniel said.

"But how do we get up there?" Kevane asked. The ceiling was pretty low, but it was still too high to reach.

"Kev," Daniel said, "you climb onto my back, and I'll boost you up. You can at least see if that's a door up there."

Kevane climbed onto Daniel, and with Daniel firmly holding his legs, he reached up and tried to push up the square area. "Hey, yeah, it gives!" Kevane cried. "It's a door, all right."

The boys moved a chair under the

trapdoor. Then, with Daniel's help, Kevane was able to push the door up and scramble through it. Once up there, Kevane lowered the ladder he found lying next to the open door. Daniel hurried up the ladder and joined his brother. He pulled the ladder back up and closed the trapdoor; if the man came back to the stained glass room soon, he wouldn't wouldn't see what had happened right away and come after them.

The boys found themselves in a tiny room. They were barely able to wave their arms around. But there was a stone stairway leading up. "This has to be the other exit," Daniel said hopefully.

The stone stairway was circular, as if they were moving up through a tower. It was very narrow and steep, and they walked carefully. Only one person at a time could walk up the steps, so Kevane walked right behind Daniel.

"This is really steep," Kevane said. The stones were rough and uneven, and any slip would be dangerous.

"Just so it leads out of here," Daniel said. He was breathing hard. Maybe the man would go into the room and see the chair sitting just under the trapdoor. Maybe he would figure out that the boys had found the trapdoor in the ceiling and were now escaping. The man had never threatened Daniel and Kevane, and he didn't even brandish a weapon. But who knew? Maybe he *was* armed. Maybe he would come charging up the steps behind them with a gun . . . Daniel couldn't be sure, so he wanted to get out of there as quickly as possible.

If this was the exit, it probably came out in the mountains. They would have a long trek back to the campsite, but at least they would be free.

"Doesn't this ever end?" Kevane groaned. Daniel could tell that his heart was pounding from the steep climb. He stopped to get his breath.

"You can't stop, Kevane," Daniel barked at him. "We have to get out before that guy realizes we're missing and takes off after us!"

Daniel figured the stairway led high up on the mountain. The tower was probably carved right from granite. As they climbed, they passed little hollowed-out spaces in the rock, niches containing carvings. Some of the carvings were jade, and some were ivory. They were mostly creatures from the zodiac, the imaginary zone in the sky where stars were arranged in 12 constellations.

"Maybe this is all a joke," Kevane said bitterly. "Maybe this stairway leads nowhere. Maybe when we get to the top, there'll be a blank wall. Maybe the old guy built this tower just to spite the world."

"No, I don't think so," Daniel said. "I think there's a purpose to it." But he was starting to wonder about the purpose himself. If this was an exit, why make it so far up and so difficult to climb?

Suddenly, a brightness began to filter down toward them. There was a bright moon in the sky, and they started to see its light.

"I think we're going to get out of here. It looks like there's a big opening up ahead!" Daniel cried.

"Man, I hope so," Kevane said, following closely behind his brother.

They began to feel cool air, and then

when they turned the last corner, they saw the open archway leading outside. There was a huge telescope mounted a few feet from the arch, perched on a rocky ledge.

"It's an observatory," Daniel said. "The old guy built the tower so he could have an observatory up here."

Daniel and Kevane stepped out onto the ledge. It was no more than 15 feet square. They were atop a large mesa. A block wall stood around the perimeter of the ledge so the astronomer peering into the telescope would not accidentally step off the ledge and plunge thousands of feet to his death.

Daniel peered over the block wall at the abyss below. Kevane joined him. Finally Kevane said, "It's a sheer cliff every which way you look. There's no way in the world we could get down from here."

"Yeah," Daniel agreed sadly.

They paced all around the ledge, shining their flashlights down to confirm what they feared. Daniel felt his sharp disappointment rise in his throat like a choking tide. He had been so sure this was the way out. When he saw the light and then felt the cool air, he thought they were minutes from freedom.

"We're outside," Kevane groaned, "but we might as well be in that underground hole! We're free, but we're not free. If we try to climb down from here, we're dead."

"I bet Overton built this so he could watch for enemy planes bringing the bomb," Daniel said.

"Yeah," Kevane said. "So what are we gonna do? We're doomed, right? We've got no choice but to go back into that crazy place."

"No. Like you said, we're outside," Daniel answered. "Maybe people are searching for us. Maybe some search planes will go over us, and we can signal them with our flashlights. They've got to be searching for us, Kevane."

"But our flashlights are getting so dim," Kevane said. "We didn't bring extra batteries. Who would've thought we'd get into something like this? Even if we did see a search plane, the flashlight beam is so weak, I bet they wouldn't even see it."

"We've got to try," Daniel said. "Maybe they would see the lights flickering."

Daniel searched the sky for signs of life. Suddenly he had a thought. "Hey," he said, "let's look into the telescope. Maybe we can see searchers looking for us."

"Good idea!" Kevane said.

Daniel looked into the telescope, but he couldn't see anything hopeful. He had read once that when someone is lost, the search parties usually look in the daylight. The terrain was rough around there, and people traveling in the darkness could easily get hurt.

"See anything?" Kevane asked.

"No," Daniel said.

"I bet that guy has figured out by now that we came up here, Dan. I bet he saw the chair positioned under the trapdoor, and he's probably on his way up with a gun," Kevane said.

"We don't know that he even has a gun," Daniel said.

"Yeah, but he's gotta be some kind of criminal," Kevane insisted. "He took over the old man's identity, and now he's hiding out. What's he hiding from? The cops, I bet."

"We don't know," Daniel insisted.

"I'm starving," Kevane said. "It doesn't seem possible that we had those big, thick steaks at noon. I'm so hungry now I could eat Aunt Clara's shepherd's pie."

Daniel shuddered at the thought of their most unfavorite food, guaranteed to be served at every family function. But he agreed, "Yeah, I'm hungry too." He figured all the exertion and stress had made them hungrier than normal.

Daniel wished he'd see a search plane. Then they could turn on their flashlights and signal it. He knew how to make a distress signal using light flashes. It was a stretch, but maybe a search plane would realize what was going on just by seeing the flashes in a place where there should be darkness.

"I hope Mom and Dad don't think we ran away," Kevane worried. "I mean, maybe they think we were so mad about Arthur joining the family that we just took off. You don't think they think that, do you?"

"Nah. They know we wouldn't do that," Daniel said.

"I'm not that much against the kid anyway," Kevane said. "I mean, sure, he's gonna be a nuisance sometimes, but that's normal. He's an okay kid. He's not real smart or good-looking or anything. He's just a kid. He sort of reminds me of myself—just an average kid. I guess that's why nobody adopted him up to now. I guess when people go looking for kids to adopt, they're looking for somebody a little special. Cute and bright. You know, if I didn't have Mom and Dad, who knows if anybody would have wanted me either."

"Most of us are just average," Daniel said. "But a lot of couples who want to adopt are looking for a baby. They don't want an older kid like Arthur. Older kids have problems. But Mom sure fell in love with Arthur. She wants him real bad."

Kevane looked up at the dark sky. "I don't see any search planes." He flicked on his flashlight. The beam was weak. "I bet that guy will be coming up here pretty soon. He's got to know where we went. What do we do if we hear him coming?"

"I don't know," Daniel said. He peered over the edge again, over the wall. "If we had ropes, we could go down like mountain climbers. They go down steeper cliffs than that."

"Yeah, but we don't have ropes, and we're not mountain climbers," Kevane said. "Maybe we should jump the guy when he shows up."

"Yeah, and then he won't ever tell us how to get out of here. Our best chance is to stay on his good side," Daniel said.

"Dan!" Kevane cried suddenly. "I hear something on the stairs. Somebody's coming. It must be him." Daniel could tell that Kevane's imagination was running away with him again. He probably imagined the wrinkled monster coming up the stairs, cudgel in hand.

"Stay cool," Daniel advised. "When he gets here, we'll tell him we were looking through the telescope, that we're interested in the stars."

"Yeah, like he's going to believe we weren't trying to escape from the madman in the underground house," Kevane sarcastically remarked.

It seemed to take forever for the man to get up the steps. But finally he appeared in the arch. The boys stood as far from the man as they could.

"What are you doing up here?" he asked.

The man stood there. And now, instead of the creepy makeup and the false wrinkles, he wore a Halloween mask where only his eyes showed—his bright, dark eyes. The ratty gray wig was gone too.

"We were, uh . . . just curious when we saw the stairs. And then we found the telescope. We like to look for planets and stuff," Daniel said.

"You were looking for a way out," the man said. "You can't wait to tell the whole world about this place."

"No, no," Daniel said. "It's a real nice observatory here. It's really exciting, you know, to look at the stars and the planets, even the moon. You can see the mountains on the moon. It's great."

Then the man said, "He watched for planes. He wrote about it in his diary.

Most nights he would come here and watch for enemy bombers containing an atomic bomb." The voice was no longer that of an old man. It was a young man's voice. It was almost a boy's voice. It sounded like someone not much older than Daniel.

"You're not an old man at all, are you?" Daniel asked. "Who are you, anyway?"

"I'm a fugitive," the young voice said. The mask looked eerie in the moonlight with its greenish glow.

Daniel went a little numb. A fugitive? That's just what he'd been afraid of. The guy was on the run from the law. He had probably escaped from prison, and he stumbled on this perfect hideout.

"You don't need to hide your face," Daniel said.

"You wouldn't want to see the real me," the man said sharply. "Believe me. I could give you nightmares like you've never had."

8 "We want out of here," Daniel said. "When are you going to end this game and let us go?"

The man said nothing for a few seconds. Then, in a less hostile voice, he said, "Let's go downstairs and have some breakfast. I'll fry eggs and sausages. Even have some pancakes."

Kevane looked hopefully at Daniel. Daniel could tell that all he wanted right now was some food. Eggs, sausages, and pancakes sounded wonderful. Kevane was even willing to postpone getting out of the underground maze if he could have something decent to eat.

"Okay, I guess," Daniel said. He couldn't tell if the guy was softening or if he was leading them to a trap. But he didn't feel they had much choice. They couldn't stay up on the observatory forever.

The boys followed the man back down the stairs in the tower. They went into the kitchen, and the man started breaking eggs into a pan on the stove. Soon the sizzle of sausages introduced a heavenly smell. Kevane could hardly stand to wait for the food.

"Who are you?" Daniel repeated the question.

"I'm a monster," he answered. "I'm a leftover from Halloween."

"Come on, no joke," Daniel said. "Who are you?"

"I'm the monster who could never find a costume as scary as himself," he said. He piled the dishes high with scrambled eggs and sausage, and then pancakes.

Kevane didn't seem to care about anything just now except attacking the food. He acted as if he'd never been so hungry in his life. Daniel decided he might as well eat too. He would probably need all the strength he could get for a showdown with this guy.

"Who's the guy in the coffin?" Daniel asked, trying another way to get at the truth.

"Ernest Abbott Overton," came the ready answer. "And once he had a decent burial, his spirit took over this place.

That's me. I'm the spirit of Mr. Overton. You guys ever see a real ghost before? Now you're looking at one."

"You're not talking to a couple of kids," Daniel snapped. "We're not buying this. Thanks for the breakfast, but we've gotta be going home now. I'm sure our parents are worried sick about us. You know how to open the door between the stained glass room and the coconut room. You could open it just like that," Daniel said, snapping his fingers.

"Okay," the man said after a pause, "let's make a deal. You pick some things you'd like to take from the stained glass room. For that, you have to promise to keep the secret about this place."

"Yeah, it's a deal," Kevane said eagerly.

"Kevane and I won't give you away once we promise not to," Daniel said. "You don't need to trade us anything for our silence. Just open that door, and we're out of here."

"Okay," the man said, "but the funny thing is, that door you're talking about is really jammed. I can't open it myself without a lot of fiddling around. I'll take you guys out the other way. Mr. Overton used this exit we'll be using most of the time. He didn't like the trapdoor. He wrote in his diary that he hated it. It was just an escape hatch in an emergency."

Daniel wasn't at all sure if the man was telling the truth or not. Maybe he was planning to lead Daniel and Kevane into some kind of trap where they'd fall over a cliff and be out of his way for good. Then he wouldn't have to worry about his secret escaping into the world.

"You sure you don't want a couple of pieces of glass?" he asked before they started out.

"No," Daniel said. He wondered now how Mr. Overton had died. Did he die of natural causes and then did this guy find and bury him? Or was this the guy who did away with poor old Overton and then put him in the box?

"So, let's go," the man said, holding a high-powered flashlight as they walked from the kitchen. He opened a door in the wall of the bedroom and said, "Here we go."

There was a tunnel before them, and the man led the way. "By the way," Daniel said, "you never did give us your name. It's kind of weird not knowing what to call you."

"You can call me by the nickname my friends at school used," he said in a strange voice. "You can call me Monty."

"How come? Is your name Montgomery or something?" Daniel asked.

"You ask too many questions," Monty said.

The tunnel had rough rock walls, and it was easy to travel. There was a slight ascent but nothing steep. Daniel couldn't imagine the job it must have been to build this place. "Boy this is some underground world," Daniel said. "Mr. Overton must have had a ton of money."

"He had plenty, yeah, but this was built over an old gold mine. A lot of the excavations had been done already when he bought the land. People thought there was a rich mother lode down here, but it was mostly a bust. Mr. Overton found it on one of his trips. Then, when he wanted a place like this, he remembered seeing the land." Monty talked about the man as if they had been close friends.

"Did you . . . uh . . . know Mr. Overton

when he was alive?" Daniel asked.

Monty did not answer right away. He stopped and turned. With the Halloween mask covering his face, Daniel couldn't tell if he was showing anger or annoyance. But when his voice came, it grated with hostility. "Oh, I get it. You're fishing around for information. I see where your little mind is going. You thought I came here looking for a place to hide, and this little old man was already here, so I had to make quick work of him, right?"

"No, no," Daniel backtracked quickly. "I just thought you know so much about Mr. Overton, maybe you were friends before he died."

"I never met him while he was alive, but I read all his diaries. He was dead a long time before I got here. I don't know how he died, but when I found his remains, he was just lying in the library like he'd fallen there. He was here alone, so there was nobody to help him, I guess. It was pretty sad. His wife had died just before he built all this. He was alone when he came to stay here," Monty said.

"It's sad for somebody to die alone like that," Kevane said.

"He was a pretty important guy in his time. I thought he deserved better than just throwing him in a hole somewhere. So I found some plywood, and I built the box and put him in it. Then I covered it with a nice velvet spread and put the stained glass angel on the top," Monty said.

"Yeah, that was a good thing to do," Daniel said uneasily. "Uh . . . he had no kids, right?"

"I told you there were no children. He left 12 thick diaries. He mostly talked about the atomic bomb and how afraid he was that the whole world would be destroyed and nobody would even know there were beautiful things in the world. That's why he created and displayed the stained glass and the coconut heads. He worked on his art while he was holed up down here. He thought there would be a few survivors, like him, and they were like keepers of civilization. He had no brothers or sisters or any living soul to care about. That's what he said. Maybe he died of loneliness . . . you think?" Monty asked, laughing then in a strange way.

Daniel got the sinking feeling that this tunnel was leading nowhere. It was another delaying action. It was a trick. Monty had no intention of letting them return to the real world.

9 Maybe Kevane had been right, Daniel thought feverishly. Maybe the two of them should just jump this guy, but then what if there *was* some trick to getting out of here? Then they'd never find it. What if they were trapped in the maze until they died too?

"Our parents are going to be really glad to see us," Daniel said, fishing for Monty's reaction. "Especially Mom. She gets really upset by things like this."

"Yeah," Kevane added. "Mom is probably so worried that she's sick. She's under a lot of stress now anyway. We're thinking about adopting this little seven-year-old kid, Arthur, and Dan and I weren't too crazy about the idea, so Mom's been trying to convince us."

Daniel figured Kevane was thinking the same thing he was. Maybe if Monty would see what nice people his parents were, he would think twice about causing them any more grief.

Monty seemed interested in Kevane's story. "So where's the kid now?" he asked.

"He's in a foster home. He's been there since he was real little. His mom died, and nobody wanted to adopt him. He's just an average kid, not exceptionally cute or smart or anything," Kevane said.

A change seemed to come over Monty. His voice turned dark and somber, almost grim. After a moment or two he said, "I grew up like that too. I was in the system."

"Oh, yeah?" Daniel said. "Then you can understand how it is for Arthur."

Monty gripped the flashlight he was carrying so tightly that the blood seemed to drain from his hand. "I had good parents," he said. "They really loved me. I know that. I had one of those baby books parents keep for their babies. They kept locks of my hair and stuff. They wrote down milestones, like when I first stood up and learned to crawl, stuff like that. They were really interested in me. But then my parents got killed in a car crash when I was two and a half, and there were no other relatives who wanted me. So I got shoved into the foster-care system."

"Must have been rough for you," Daniel said sympathetically, eager to stay on the guy's good side now that they were maybe on their way out of this place.

"Nobody ever loved me again," Monty said in a bitter voice. "Nobody."

Daniel didn't know what to say. He cleared his throat nervously. Then finally he said, "Well, you're a young guy. You've got plenty of time to get your own family, and then it'll all be different, you know?"

Monty laughed sardonically. Then, still gripping the flashlight, he continued his story. "I don't remember the first foster homes. It's all a blur. But I think I must have been a problem kid because nobody kept me for long. Then, when I was about six, they put me with this family, the Randalls. They had two kids of their own. They took me in for the money the system paid them. They were always mad at me. I remember that. I caused them a lot of trouble. They hated me and I hated them . . ."

"Must've been hard," Kevane said.

As he listened, Daniel wondered if they were actually getting closer to the exit or if Monty was leading them in circles. There was no way to tell.

"There was a fire," Monty said, stopping to take a deep breath. "They got out, the Randalls did, and they got their kids out. They said I started the fire playing with matches. I don't know if I did or not. Anyway, by the time the fireman got me out, I was burned real bad."

"That's awful," Daniel said.

"I was in the hospital for a long time. I never went back to the Randalls. I got in some other foster homes, and I was in school by then. I was scarred, see, and some of the kids teased me about it. Sometimes they called me Monty, you know. That was their nickname for me. It was short for *monster*. That's what I was—a monster. An ugly, scarred monster. I laughed along with them sometimes and made monster noises because I didn't know what else to do. Getting mad only made it worse. But then when I got older, I got even. I slashed the tires on their cars, and I stole stuff. I broke into their houses when their parents were on vacation, and I trashed everything."

Daniel and Kevane exchanged worried looks. Where was all this going? Had the guy killed some of his tormentors? Could he be a murderer on the run?

If that was so, then the boys had little chance of getting out of there.

Monty went on in his bitter voice, "Finally the cops caught me. I got off the first time, but then I stole more stuff. I got into bad fights. They got me again and sent me to this youth camp in the mountains. I was supposed to learn to be a good citizen taking care of the trees, but one day I just ran from the work detail, and they never caught me. That was a couple of years ago. I ran and ran, and then I found the trapdoor. I came down those steps like you guys did. I found the coconut heads and the stained glass room . . . and the bones of the old man. I sort of became the curator of his bomb shelter, right?" He laughed shortly.

"What are you, about 18?" Daniel asked. "You're only a couple years older than me."

"Yeah," Monty admitted.

"You shouldn't be holed up here like that old man was. You're a guy with your whole life in front of you. You can get those troubles with the law straightened out, and then you'll be free. You can live your life in the open," Daniel said.

"You don't know what you're talking about," Monty snapped. He quickened the pace. Daniel was getting a little short of breath. The tunnel was going up now. They were climbing higher into the mountains. That didn't make sense. Maybe they'd end up at another ledge like the observatory, a place with no escape. Maybe Monty planned to get them there and leave them stranded. Maybe he hoped they'd try to climb out and get killed in the effort. Then he wouldn't have to do them in himself.

"How much farther?" Daniel asked.

"About a mile," Monty said.

"I hope we can call our parents right away. They must be really going crazy with worry by now," Daniel said. "They probably think we drowned in that big lake we saw." Daniel glanced at his watch. It was 8:30 in the morning. Another day. It seemed so long ago that they had been at camp with their parents, but it was only yesterday.

Monty didn't say anything. He just kept walking. He led the way, sweeping his flashlight beam before them like a glowing broom.

Then Daniel heard the sound of water. Maybe there was a waterfall or a river ahead. Maybe it was an exit, but you'd need a boat to get across and no boat would be there. Maybe Monty would try to shove them into the rapids.

Daniel grabbed Kevane's arm and whispered, "Be careful. I don't know what he's got up his sleeve, so don't let him get behind you or anything."

Kevane nodded. Daniel knew he was thinking the same dark thoughts.

"What's that?" Monty asked, looking back at them.

"Oh, I was just telling Kevane to watch his step if we got near any water."

"There's a stream ahead. Mr. Overton built a little drawbridge across it. You can pull the bridge back so nobody can cross over. It was another way he tried to protect himself. He got real suspicious toward the end. It was kind of sad," Monty said. "He got pretty paranoid. He figured that with the bombs starting to fall, people would try to storm his shelter, and then there wouldn't be room enough for him and everybody else or supplies enough . . ."

"Poor guy," Daniel said. "He must have been miserable. That's no way to live."

"I don't know," Monty said. "I kind of know where he was coming from. This is a good, safe place. Bad stuff can't get you here. Nothing but a few mice and the birds. They're better than people. They don't make fun of you. They don't look at you with disgust. You toss them a few crumbs and they're your buddies."

Daniel's heart raced when he noticed the tunnel getting lighter. Daylight was ahead, all right. But would Monty let them cross the bridge and escape? Would he trust them to keep his secret? Or would he find a way to make sure his secret never got out?

Suddenly sunlight was streaming all around them. An iron gate barred their way outside, an iron gate with a padlock on it. Daniel was so scared he could hardly breathe.

10 Monty stuck a key in the padlock, and it snapped open. He then swung the gate.

The stream Monty had described was a rushing river. It stood between them and the meadow below—and freedom.

Monty turned his back to the two boys for a moment, and when he turned again, he wasn't wearing the Halloween mask.

Daniel stared at the young man before him, burn scars ravaging his left cheek. It was very shocking at first, but it was the kind of thing you got used to and eventually hardly noticed.

"Now you see why I can't leave here," Monty cried. "Why I can't go back to the world and live a normal life."

"It's not as bad as you think it is," Daniel said. "You've let it get too big in your own mind. If you came with us to camp, our mom and dad would welcome you. Nobody would care about the scar."

Monty stared at Daniel in stunned

confusion. Daniel knew he had expected the sight of his burned face to shock and revolt the boys. He had expected to see horror in their faces.

"Why are you lying to me?" he cried. "I'm a monster. Anybody would get sick just looking at me!"

"You're wrong," Daniel said. "You're like Mr. Overton. You're a prisoner of your own fears. You don't want to end up like he did—a bag of bones in a cave. You deserve better, man."

"Yeah," Kevane joined in. "There are a lot of guys at school who look different. Maybe they don't have scars, but they've got funny chins or big noses. None of us are perfect!"

Monty went to the controls of the drawbridge, and soon it spanned the raging waters.

"Get out of here before I change my mind," Monty said. Daniel had the terrible fear that before they got to the other side of the bridge, Monty would yank at the controls and dump them into the river. So he grabbed Kevane by the shirt and sprinted quickly across the bridge, leaping to solid ground on the other side.

Daniel turned then and looked back. "We won't give your secret away. We swear it. We'll just tell them we got lost in the woods. But listen to me. There's a big world out there. You'll do okay. Don't do like the old man did and die in the dark. Don't get buried before you're dead, okay?"

Monty stood there, a strange and confused look on his face. Then he shouted, "Do me a favor?"

"Yeah, anything," Daniel said.

"Tell your folks to take the kid. Adopt Arthur. Give the kid a home," Monty shouted.

Daniel grinned. "You got it," he shouted back. Then he added, "When you get ready to leave the bunker, Monty, give us a call." Daniel called out their phone number in Woodland Hills.

Then Kevane said, "If you forget the number, we're in the phone directory. Cyrus and Emilie Robinson on Rios Street."

Monty smiled. He actually smiled. And Daniel thought that he didn't look bad at all with a smile on his face.

The boys reached a trail in minutes and called their parents from a ranger station about a mile from the underground bunker.

After Daniel assured their parents they were okay, Kevane grabbed the phone. "Hey, you guys. We want to take Arthur. Daniel and I decided, okay? If you guys still want Arthur, we're all for it."

Their mom was crying, Daniel could tell, when Kevane handed him back the phone. "We thought we'd lost our two boys," she said, "but now we've gotten you back and another son as well!"

Daniel thought he'd tell his parents later on about an interesting guy he'd met on their vacation, a kid with a scarred face. Daniel figured he'd better mention Monty because deep in his heart he thought Monty might show up at the Robinson house for a visit.

Daniel hoped he would, anyway.